C000089418

1,000,000 Books

are available to read at

www.ForgottenBooks.com

Read online
Download PDF
Purchase in print

ISBN 978-0-260-96576-9
PIBN 11111165

This book is a reproduction of an important historical work. Forgotten Books uses
state-of-the-art technology to digitally reconstruct the work, preserving the original format
whilst repairing imperfections present in the aged copy. In rare cases, an imperfection in
the original, such as a blemish or missing page, may be replicated in our edition. We do,
however, repair the vast majority of imperfections successfully; any imperfections that
remain are intentionally left to preserve the state of such historical works.

Forgotten Books is a registered trademark of FB &c Ltd.
Copyright © 2018 FB &c Ltd.
FB &c Ltd, Dalton House, 60 Windsor Avenue, London, SW19 2RR.
Company number 08720141. Registered in England and Wales.

For support please visit www.forgottenbooks.com

1 MONTH OF
FREE
READING

at

www.ForgottenBooks.com

By purchasing this book you are eligible for one month membership to ForgottenBooks.com, giving you unlimited access to our entire collection of over 1,000,000 titles via our web site and mobile apps.

To claim your free month visit:

www.forgottenbooks.com/free1111165

* Offer is valid for 45 days from date of purchase. Terms and conditions apply.

English
Français
Deutsche
Italiano
Español
Português

www.forgottenbooks.com

Mythology Photography **Fiction**
Fishing Christianity **Art** Cooking
Essays Buddhism Freemasonry
Medicine **Biology** Music **Ancient
Egypt** Evolution Carpentry Physics
Dance Geology **Mathematics** Fitness
Shakespeare **Folklore** Yoga Marketing
Confidence Immortality Biographies
Poetry **Psychology** Witchcraft
Electronics Chemistry History **Law**
Accounting **Philosophy** Anthropology
Alchemy Drama Quantum Mechanics
Atheism Sexual Health **Ancient History**
Entrepreneurship Languages Sport
Paleontology Needlework Islam
Metaphysics Investment Archaeology
Parenting Statistics Criminology
Motivational

The

By JOHN F. GORDON

CHALLENGE
of the MARKET PLACE

By FREDERIC G. DONNER

From the collection of the

The fir  In 1900.

San Francisco, California
2008

Remarks made at the GM Motorama
Luncheon for Business Leaders
New York City, October 31, 1960

MODEL CHANGE

JOHN F. GORDON
President

A demonstration used in the 1900 Auto Show to prove that the automobile would operate and could be controlled.

The automobile show is a great tradition in our industry. The first one was held here in New York at old Madison Square Garden in 1900. Cars were actually driven around the sawdust ring — to prove, I suppose, that they really could run.

Since then we have had many auto shows — industry shows and company shows like our own Motoramas. These shows are always timed to coincide with new-model introductions, and because of that fact we feel they have done a great deal to spark progress in our industry — giving us a cutoff point, a deadline when we had to be ready with new and better cars and trucks.

I know that some people sincerely disapprove of our practice of coming out with new models each year. They believe it would be better for the customer, for the economy, for the manufacturer and even for his employes to stick with the same models over a period of years and only make changes when

3

The first Automobile Show was held in New York in 1900.

Remarks made at the GM Motorama
Luncheon for Business Leaders
New York City, October 31, 1960

JOHN F. GORDON
President

A demonstration used in the 1900 Auto Show to prove that the automobile would operate and could be controlled.

The automobile show is a great tradition in our industry. The first one was held here in New York at old Madison Square Garden in 1900. Cars were actually driven around the sawdust ring — to prove, I suppose, that they really could run.

Since then we have had many auto shows — industry shows and company shows like our own Motoramas. These shows are always timed to coincide with new-model introductions, and because of that fact we feel they have done a great deal to spark progress in our industry — giving us a cutoff point, a deadline when we had to be ready with new and better cars and trucks.

I know that some people sincerely disapprove of our practice of coming out with new models each year. They believe it would be better for the customer, for the economy, for the manufacturer and even for his employes to stick with the same models over a period of years and only make changes when

3

The Car That Marks My Limit

By R. E. Olds, Designer

I have no quarrel with men who ask more for their cars—none with men who ask less. I have only to say that, after 25 years —after creating 24 models and building tens of thousands of cars—*here's the best I know.* I call it My Farewell Car.

I claim for this car no great innovation. The time is past for that.

Thousands of good men, for two decades, have worked at perfecting cars. No man can ever go much further than the best these men have done.

I believe that Reo the Fifth, in every feature, shows the utmost these men have accomplished. It represents, in addition, the best I have learned through 25 years of continuous striving. So it comes, I believe, pretty close to finality.

... what can be done by

Myriads of cars used by myriads of owners have taught me every possible weakness. They have shown the need for big margins of safety, for exactness, for careful inspection, for laboratory tests.

I Go to Extremes

For every part I know the best steel alloy. To make sure that I get it, I analyze all my steel.

I built a crushing machi... 50 tons' capacity just ...
gears.

My

The wheel base is long, the wheels are large, the car is over-tired. I avoid all the petty economies

New Center Control

The gear shifting is done by that center "cane-handle." It moves only three inches in each of four directions to change to every speed and reverse.

There are no side levers. Both of the brakes, also the clutch, ar operated by the f...

initial price of $1,055 is t imum. It is based on low cost for materials, ured on a doubled out to this new creation.

If costs advance our p advance. But we shal this low just as lo sible. Tha than m

---

we have major engineering advances to offer.

My question to these skeptics is: If this were done, would our industry produce as many new product improvements as it does?

Back in 1912 Mr. R. E. Olds published an ad that has become a classic in automobile circles. "My farewell car," the ad proclaimed. "I do not believe that a car materially better will ever be built."

What if all manufacturers had adopted this attitude back in 1912? If they had, I am afraid the horse would have continued to be a serious competitor to what would still be our chugging roadsters and bouncing touring cars.

Obviously, this never could have happened.

Automobiles have the stamina, dependability, comfort, safety, maneuverability and eye appeal they now possess precisely because we know it is always possible to build a better car. Our designers and engineers are kept close to the boiling point by the knowledge that if they don't perfect power steering or some equally significant improvement right away some competitor will.

It is clear to me that new car buyers have benefited tremendously over the years from what has been termed planned obsolescence but which we think is more accurately called dynamic obsolescence.

But new car customers are not the only ones to gain from dynamic obsolescence. They are a minority because only about half as many cars are bought

CUSTOMERS GET BETTER CARS

new as are bought used. If our new car customers did not trade in their old cars with lots of mileage still in them, thousands of your neighbors and mine would probably be riding to work and market on bicycles, as is the case today in many countries.

Does a car cost more because millions of dollars are spent in tooling up for new models? At first blush it might seem so, but let's analyze what happens.

If manufacturers did not change models each year, the 20 million new car buyers who now come to market over a period of three years might well come to market once in six years. In other words, they would continue to use the same car as long as it gave satisfactory service. There would be no incentive to replace it. Obviously, this would cut our annual sales in half. With volume reduced, each car would cost more to produce, and I am sure that this increased cost would be sufficient to more than offset any saving resulting from not changing models.

Businessmen long ago learned that it is sound economics to tear down an old building and replace it with a new one. We have learned to apply this

HIGHER VOLUME KEEPS PRICES DOWN

6

same principle to our business, except that we do not tear down.

We not only build more and better new cars and make millions of used cars available; we also provide better jobs for more people.

I know that some of you are thinking: "But there are a few cars which succeed without changing models every year."

This is true precisely because there are only a few such cars. An annual market of six million new cars can support a few cars whose appearance and design remain static over fairly long periods. But, if all manufacturers followed suit, demand would fall off, fewer cars would be produced and unit costs would increase. Most of our business comes from old customers who are repeat buyers. If we had nothing new to offer, these customers would come back less frequently. Even a reduced price would not tempt them, any more than you would be tempted to replace your electric razor if you were told you could now buy it for 80 per cent of the price originally paid.

1927 *PONTIAC*

1961 *PONTIAC*

I am devoting most of my time this afternoon to discussing dynamic obsolescence because the process seems to be so widely misunderstood. Neither our industry, nor any other industry for that matter, need apologize for dynamic obsolescence. It makes a substantial contribution to our economy and to our customers.

It is true that automotive progress on the whole has evolved gradually from year to year. Changes in performance may not be radical in every year, but over a period of years they add up. To convince yourself of this, just drive a 1955 car and compare it with the 1961 model.

Although in any one year changes may not appear on the surface to be substantial, as a matter of fact they are always a lot more substantial than the public realizes. It is hard to glamorize an improved steel, a new method of chromium plating or a changed frame design. Yet there are literally hundreds of such beneath-the-surface changes each year. A car is like an iceberg in this respect, and it is the sum of these unseen subsurface changes that gives our customers the improved ride, performance and reliability that we talk about in our advertising.

To pick just one example, in the last five years our engineers have so improved the design and construction of brake drums that the temperature generated when you apply your brakes has been reduced by as much as 200 degrees. These new cooler brakes are much more efficient and more dependable than the old brakes, and they last longer.

This year, of course, in addition to such evolutionary changes in our regular lines of cars, our 1961 introductions include three new smaller series — the Buick Special, the Oldsmobile F-85 and the Pontiac Tempest.

Each of these new series of cars, plus the expanded Chevrolet Corvair series, represents a sound approach to meeting the demand for smaller cars. I won't say that they give you all that a large car does, because that would be obviously untrue, but I do say that they offer remarkable performance and comfort for their area of the market.

So I invite you to come and see these new cars, and also all of our other products which we have brought together in typical Motorama settings.

We can truthfully say, with Mr. Olds, that these are the finest creations we have ever built. We cannot say with him, however, that we do not believe cars materially better ever will be built.

For this is and will continue to be our objective: each year to strive to build better and better products to the benefit of ourselves, our customers and the economy.

FREDERIC G. DONNER
Chairman of the Board

For American business, the important challenge of the future is the steadily intensifying competition for the consumer's dollar.

Competition to gain the favor of the consumer has always been keen. But today's competition is broader and tougher.

It is broader because today's consumer can choose from a wider variety of products and services. It is tougher because of the great advances in technology.

For us in the automobile business the challenge of the market place is one that calls for all our skills in design, in production, in marketing. It calls for

spending large sums of money and for taking risks without any certainty of earning a profit. It calls for bold planning here at home and on a world-wide basis. It calls, above all, for optimism and for faith in the future growth of this country and the world.

10

Jack Gordon has told you why the annual model change is desirable. I want to discuss the results of the annual model change as they are embodied in our 1961 lines of cars.

The automobile industry is now passing through another of those dramatic stages that have characterized its evolution and growth over the years. We have been witnessing a series of changes which may prove little short of revolutionary over the long term. They represent, as often has been the case before, the constructive adaptation of cars to the demonstrated needs and desires of our customers.

The challenge is to provide the American buyer on an economical basis with a widening range of product choices. Within the limit imposed by volume requirements, we are tailoring our products in a greater variety of ways to meet the needs of individual customers. We are giving the American consumer a wide variety to choose from at every price.

In 1955, when car sales reached a new high, 98 per cent of the industry's volume was accounted for by standard size domestic cars. The balance of 2 per cent, representing fewer than 150,000 cars, included some 45 foreign and smaller domestic lines. Even as recently as three years ago, standard size cars still accounted for 95 per cent of the total market. Foreign imports had then reached 4 per cent of the total, with the balance of 1 per cent being domestic smaller cars.

In 1957 it was far from certain that the demand for smaller cars would grow. Yet it was even earlier that this new trend was recognized by General Motors and the designs for our smaller cars were being initiated. The design of the Corvair, introduced by Chevrolet a year ago, was finalized by mid-1957.

For the 1961 model year, four lines of smaller cars are being offered by General Motors, including the new lines now being introduced by Buick, Oldsmobile and Pontiac. This range of offerings becomes even more attractive from the customer's standpoint when we consider that these lines supplement a continuing wide range of standard size cars.

The new smaller General Motors cars incorporate engineering and design innovations that were developed over a period of years. Tooling was ap-

**A CAR FOR EVERY
PURSE AND PURPOSE**

proved early in 1959, reflecting the lead time of two to three years required to engineer and tool today's modern cars. Except for minor changes, we were committed to the 1961 programs well before the 1960 lines were introduced a year ago.

Our 1961 cars reflect, therefore, our evaluation — made in 1958 and 1959 — of what American consumers would want in 1961. We have expanded the number of body styles available in the Corvair line to take full advantage of the car's unusual design characteristics. Each of the new smaller cars being introduced by Buick, Oldsmobile and Pontiac offers customers an exceptional and attractive combination of styling and mechanical features. Each represents the imaginative translation of market trends into a distinctive product.

These four smaller cars bring the best of General Motors engineering know-how to the requirements of smaller size and lighter weight. Extensive use of aluminum, new positioning of engine and transmission components and a number of other significant engineering advances have made it possible for us to build into these cars low price and economy and yet retain American standards of performance, size and comfort. We have thus adapted the small car concept to American needs and standards.

Every automobile represents a balancing of choices which must be made by designers, engineers and production men. In the case of our larger cars, it is possible to offer more in terms of greater comfort, increased space, improved ride stability, better handling and stepped-up engine performance. Because of these advantages, we expect that the majority of our customers will continue to purchase our larger cars.

This does not mean, however, that we must not continue to anticipate changes in customer preference in the future. To meet the challenge of the market place, we must recognize changes in customer needs and desires far enough ahead to have the right products in the right places at the right time and in the right quantity.

We must balance trends in preference against the many compromises that are necessary to make a final product that is both reliable and good looking, that performs well and that sells at a competitive price in the necessary volume. We must design, not just the cars we would like to build, but more importantly, the cars that our customers want to buy.

The pressures of a competitive market also require that we be ever alert to opportunities that will enable us to lower manufacturing costs. We must constantly seek to improve materials, methods and processes and make the most of technological advances. We must also assure ourselves that we will have the plant capacity to produce the volume demanded by the market with sufficient flexibility to respond to shifts in customer tastes and preferences.

But competition is not alone a matter of good design and efficient production. We cannot assume that a better car will sell itself, or that the customer will automatically beat a path to the dealer's door. Whether the customer feels it is worth his time to visit the dealer showroom and see our products depends upon how well we as the manufacturer have succeeded in stimulating his interest. Alert and aggressive merchandising is required to make the customer aware of what we have to offer. The Motorama is just one example — but we think a dramatic one — of how we bring our cars and other products to the attention of the customer and meet the challenge of a growing market.

That the automobile market is indeed a growing one cannot be questioned. Before the war, demand for cars averaged well under 4 million units annually. In recent years we have moved up to a level that has fluctuated around 6 million cars a year. I am convinced that we are now approaching a new sales level of 7 million cars annually.

As a matter of fact, if consumer incomes continue to rise and consumer confidence is sustained, sales of domestic and foreign built passenger cars should reach a level of 7 million units in 1961. Certainly the domestic industry, with its expanded lines of cars covering a broader range of prices, is in an excellent position to achieve the maximum volume which the country's general levels of income and employment can support.

We in General Motors recognize that a good automobile year has to be built on a foundation of generally good business conditions. Our forward planning is based on the expectation that new car demand may reach the 7 million car level. It is our

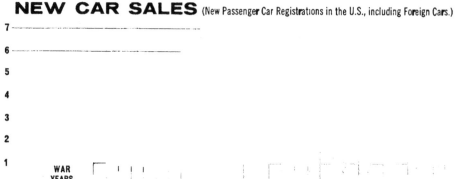

NEW CAR SALES (New Passenger Car Registrations in the U.S., including Foreign Cars.)

job to be ready to build all the cars the market will want. This we are prepared to do. Our success will be measured by the results, and not by forecasts.

In contrast to year-to-year changes in demand, which cannot be forecast precisely, the vigorous long-term growth of the automobile industry is assured. Our population will continue to grow. There will be further improvement in productivity and in personal incomes. The movement to the suburbs will continue.

Already almost 30 per cent of all families live in suburban areas, and it is a striking fact that the number of cars owned per household in suburbs is nearly one-half greater than in cities and about one-third above that of the remainder of the United States.

As the general level of income rises and as the need for cars increases, more families will be able to afford and will decide to buy new cars. More families will want and be able to own two or more cars.

In the next 10 years, we look for a growth of about

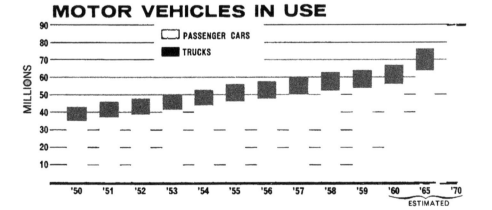

MOTOR VEHICLES IN USE

40 per cent in the number of passenger cars in use, bringing the total to 75 million cars at the end of the decade. With trucks added, there will be 90 million vehicles on the road. Participation in this growth of the market is our great challenge in the years ahead.

Prospects for growth are by no means confined to this country. In 1950, for example, about 2 million passenger cars were on the road in the six countries which now comprise the European Common Market.

Today there are 11½ million cars in use — almost 6 times as many. The rise in car ownership in the seven European Free Trade countries has also been striking — from 3 million in 1950 to about 8 million today. Within the past decade, sales of passenger cars in overseas markets have increased steadily and in recent years have approached the totals of our domestic market.

What this has meant to overseas economies is clearly evident. The bicycle rack is being replaced by the parking lot. Highways are being improved. Motor trips to vacation resorts have become popular.

Camping and camp sites are commonplace, as people of all nationalities travel the length and breadth of Europe.

Continued growth in these overseas markets is certain. Despite the striking rise of the past 10 years, today's levels of car ownership, measured in terms of cars per 1,000 of population, are about those reached by the United States in the early Twenties. The formation of the Common Market and the European Free Trade Association has opened up enlarged opportunities for all producers located in these trading areas. Our long-range estimates indicate that demand for passenger cars in markets outside the United States will approach 8 million units annually by 1970. Demand for trucks, which is expected to show an even more rapid growth, should then reach nearly $2\frac{1}{2}$ million units, bringing the combined overseas demand by 1970 to about $10\frac{1}{2}$ million cars and trucks a year for the free world.

The types of cars in demand overseas can be satisfied only in small part by the cars that the American market wants and requires. Lower levels of income abroad, very high gasoline prices and automobile taxes which rise sharply with engine size all contribute to customer acceptance of low-powered, small and light cars. Shorter traveling distances also help to make the performance of such cars acceptable.

In those countries having their own automobile industry, it is natural for customers to be favorably disposed to local products. This tendency has been significantly strengthened in many countries by the necessity of husbanding foreign exchange and of providing local industry with a home market. In some countries, outside competition has also been discouraged by the establishment of restrictive quotas and the imposition of very high import surcharges.

General Motors has been exporting cars and trucks to overseas markets since 1911. These exports reached their highest levels thirty years ago. While we have continued to merchandise the American product aggressively abroad, it early became evident that if General Motors were to participate fully in these expanding overseas markets, it would have to become a part of them.

Our present position overseas reflects a philosophy that has guided our planning over the past 35 to 40 years. Our objective has been and is to serve our overseas customers through operations established as an integral part of the overseas economies in which they are located. This we have done by establishing manufacturing and assembly plants abroad. Today almost 90 per cent of the vehicles we sell overseas are produced in our overseas manufacturing plants.

We began to manufacture cars in England in 1925. We have produced cars in Germany since 1929 and in Australia since the end of World War II. We are now producing more than 750,000 cars and trucks a year in these countries. A truck manufacturing plant was completed in Brazil in 1959 and a new truck plant is being built in Argentina.

We have been expanding our overseas facilities rapidly and have recently announced further major expansions in several countries to be made over the next two years. In Western Germany, for example, the development of a large and entirely new manufacturing plant in the Ruhr area to supplement our present Opel facilities has been announced. Expansion programs are also under way in England and Australia. These developments will greatly increase our capacity in these countries to produce for the overseas markets.

At the close of 1949 our total overseas assets amounted to about $350,000,000. This has increased by $1,000,000,000 and now amounts to $1,350,000,-000. We are projecting that within the next two years alone, on the basis of our present expansion plans, further expenditures of $500,000,000 for plant, equipment and tooling will be required for our manufacturing and assembly facilities in 19 countries overseas. With these expenditures, General Motors will be well prepared to participate aggressively in the major overseas trading areas.

Here at home the continuing challenge of the market place has called for equally bold action. Each year it is necessary to spend large amounts for plant, machinery, equipment and tooling. We must bring out our new models each year; we must assure ourselves of adequate capacity to keep pace with the market for our products; and we must keep our plants efficient and up to date.

These are necessities which are ever with us. They involve risks which cannot be avoided and which are implicit in an aggressive anticipation of consumer needs and desires.

This year — 1960 — is no exception. To introduce our new models and for the other essential purposes I have mentioned, we are spending at home and abroad approximately $1,200,000,000.

Looking to the future, we are continuing to plan for a strong and growing market. Only in this way can we progress. In 1961, for plant, machinery, equipment and tooling, we plan to spend about $1,250,000,000 in this country and overseas.

This, we submit, demonstrates our confidence in our economy and in this great industry of ours. It is the best kind of evidence of our belief in our ability to meet the challenge of the market place. The $1,250,000,000 investment that we will be making in 1961 testifies to our faith in the continued economic progress of this country and of the free world as a whole, and in the continued demand for the products we manufacture.

We foresee for General Motors a decade of profitable growth through our participation in the expanding markets at home and abroad.

By 1970 we can anticipate a total demand for passenger cars in the free world in the neighborhood of 16 million units. Demand for trucks will reach nearly 4 million units. On this basis total worldwide demand for passenger cars and trucks may be about 20 million vehicles a year by 1970.

We will build cars and trucks in the United States for the home market and for those markets that want American-type cars, and we will continue our long-time policy of building cars abroad for sale in the overseas markets.

This is the story, in brief, of what our **Motorama** is all about. This is the challenge of the market place — world wide — in the Sixties. It is a challenge to grow. It is a challenge to design well and produce efficiently the kinds of cars our customers want to buy. It is a challenge to market our products with all the skill at our command.

We accept this challenge. We propose to meet it. In doing so we shall serve not only our customers and the public but our employes and stockholders as well.

CPSIA information can be obtained
at www.ICGtesting.com
Printed in the USA
LVHW021509261118
598291LV00012B/1211

9 780260 965769